Published by Creative Education
123 South Broad Street, Mankato, Minnesota 56001
Creative Education is an imprint of The Creative Company

Designed by Stephanie Blumenthal
Production Design by Tamarin Graphics

Photographs by Richard Cummins

Library of Congress Cataloging-in-Publication Data

Cummins, Richard.
Ireland / by Richard Cummins
p. cm. — (Let's Investigate)
Includes glossary and index
Summary: Examines the history, landscape, wildlife, structures,
people, economy, and weather of Ireland.
ISBN 1-58341-032-5
1. Ireland—Juvenile literature. [1. Ireland.] I. Title.
II. Series: Let's Investigate (Mankato, Minn.)
DA906.C86   2000
941.5—dc21   99-29916

First edition

2 4 6 8 9 7 5 3 1

IRELAND

RICHARD CUMMINS

Creative Education

IRISH

Ireland is the most westerly nation in Europe, and Slea Head in county Kerry is Ireland's most westerly point.

***Above, the Causeway coastline in Northern Ireland
Right, Dunguaire Castle in county Galway, Ireland***

hen thinking of Ireland, many people think of green fields, stone fences, rain, leprechauns, and people living in thatched cottages. Some of these things are true—or are based in truth—but in reality there's a lot more to this beautiful nation. Today, Ireland has managed to combine Stone Age history with modern high-tech knowledge, forming one of Europe's most successful nations.

IRISH
HISTORY

The founder of the American Navy, Commodore John Barry, was an Irishman from Wexford town.

LANDSCAPE AND WILDLIFE

Millions of tourists visit Ireland each year, mostly during the warmer summer months. They love to see the colorful villages, castles, and beautiful landscape. One of the most popular places of interest is the Giant's Causeway in Northern Ireland. The causeway was formed when a lava flow cooled quickly and formed thousands of columns with hexagonal shapes. The columns reach up to 20 inches (50 cm) in diameter and up to 20 feet (6 m) in height.

Clonakilty town, located in county Cork

The Island of Staffa in Scotland has a similar formation. Some explain this strange formation with the legend of a giant who laid the columns to make a path that would lead across the sea to Scotland.

The landscape is one of Ireland's greatest attractions. It varies from **bogs** and lakes in the central lowlands to mountains and rocky islands in the west. Between these two extremes, the island has abundant lush, green pasture land, the result of plentiful rainfall.

IRISH
SEA

The Irish Sea, the body of water separating Scotland from Northern Ireland, is only 11 miles (18 km) wide at its narrowest point.

Street signs in Kenmare town, county Kerry

IRISH LIGHT

The oldest lighthouse in Ireland is Hook Head in county Wexford. Built in 1172, it is one of the world's oldest working lighthouses.

The heron is a bird that is native to the area on the River Shannon

Oak woodland, which once covered much of the country, survives only in Killarney National Park and in a few isolated mountain valleys. Wildlife in Ireland is limited. The only reptile is a small lizard; larger mammals include deer, the pine martin, fox, badger, squirrel, and hare. Sea birds are plentiful on the coast along with gray seals. The pheasant, heron, and swan are the largest of the inland birds.

P eat land, or bogs, as they are called in Ireland, were formed over millions of years and cover large areas of land. They are useless for farming but provide an important source of peat fuel. The wet turf (as peat is called locally) is cut by hand and set in stacks to dry, then burned for heating in the winter months. Efforts are now underway to preserve the remaining bogs, as they provide a unique habitat for rare plants and insects.

IRISH
N A M E

Ireland earned the nickname "The Emerald Isle" for its lush green landscape.

9

Sea birds called gannets (left) and seals (above) inhabit many smaller islands of Ireland

IRISH
POLICE

The police in Ireland are one of only a few police forces in the world who do not carry guns.

Above, Kylemore Lake in county Mayo
Right, Ess-Na-Laragh Waterfall in Glenariff Forest Park in county Antrim, Northern Ireland
Opposite, bog lilies

THE CLIMATE

The Irish **climate** is mild in comparison to the United States. Temperatures in the winter months generally drop to around 40°F (4°C), and snow is rare, except on the higher mountains of the northwest. Summer temperatures rarely exceed 70°F (20°C). Ireland has one of the wettest climates in western Europe with an average rainfall of 50 to 100 inches (127-254 cm) a year, creating a lush and green landscape. Rain falls throughout the year, and a typical day has brief rain showers.

IRISH HISTORY

*The cities of Dublin, Waterford, and Limerick were founded by **Vikings** who came to Ireland hundreds of years ago.*

A single standing stone in the Nire Valley (above) and a formation called the Derrintaggart West Stone Circle (right)

HISTORIC STRUCTURES

The ancient stone structures found all over Ireland are known as **megaliths**. They were built during the early Bronze Age as religious sites, **astronomical calendars**, and graves. There are four different types of these formations: standing stones, stone rows, stone circles, and burial chambers. Many of these structures still exist today because people have left them alone—damaging them is said to bring bad luck.

13

The most well-known structure is the Portal Dolmen burial chamber found on the Burren limestone plateau. In the late eighth century, Vikings from Scandinavia began to raid Ireland. Monks in the monasteries built round towers for defense from these raiders. Round towers were usually 100 feet (30 m) tall, and the door was located 13 feet (4 m) above ground level.

Remains of an ancient round tower called Cloigtheach in Inishmore, part of Ireland's Aran Islands

IRISH
LEGEND

An old legend says that kissing the Blarney Stone gives you the gift of story-telling. The stone is found on top of an ancient ruined cas-tle. Visitors must lie on their backs and lean upside-down to kiss it.

A standing round tower in Ardmore, county Waterford

The only way into these towers was by using a wooden ladder. During attacks, the monks would take religious manuscripts and other valuables into the towers, pulling up the ladders and staying there until the Vikings left. In 1014, the Irish, led by King Brian Boru, defeated the Vikings at the Battle of Clontarf. Ireland's conflict didn't end, though. Hundreds of castles were built over the centuries by different armies who occupied the country for various periods of time.

While many castles are now in ruins, a few are still lived in. They were built for defense on hills overlooking the surrounding countryside. Some have been restored and turned into houses, hotels, and tourist attractions. The most visited castle is Bunratty in county Limerick, which has been restored to look as it did when first lived in during the 15th century. The Rock of Cashel is the most impressive castle in the country, perched high on top of a hill overlooking the town of Cashel.

IRISH MONEY

The official currency of Ireland is the punt. In the 1990s, Ireland made plans to join the rest of the **European Community** *in using a single currency for all nations: the euro.*

Above, Irish money
Left, Johnstown Castle
in county Wexford

IRISH
BELIEF

Ireland has no snakes, which led to the legend that Saint Patrick, the patron saint of Ireland, chased them all into the sea. St. Patrick's Day is dedicated to him and is celebrated in many nations on March 17.

Above, Irish sheep Center, the remains of Hore Abbey in Cashel town, county Tipperary

In the fifth century the castle was the home of the kings of Munster. In 1101 they gave it to a church, and it became a religious center. Within the castle walls are a round tower, cathedral, chapel, and graveyard.

Thatched cottages are a common feature of the landscape and are more often found in the Republic of Ireland than in Northern Ireland. Thatched roofs are made of reeds harvested from river banks. The reeds are dried and tied to the roof by ropes. The thatch, which rots, is replaced every 7 to 10 years.

THE LAND AND ITS PEOPLE

Ireland is a small island, only 150 miles (241 km) wide and 350 miles (563 km) in length. This is about half the size of the state of New York.

The Republic of Ireland (Eire) covers 83 percent of the island of Ireland. The island is divided into 32 counties, 26 of which form the Republic. The remaining six northeastern counties form Northern Ireland—part of the **United Kingdom**.

IRISH
SHIP

The famous ocean liner "Titanic" was built in the Belfast shipyards. It was called the unsinkable ship, but it sank on its maiden voyage in 1912 when it struck an iceberg.

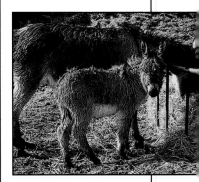

Donkeys are a common sight on Irish farms

IRISH
FLAG

The flag of the Irish Republic consists of three equal vertical stripes in green, white, and gold.

The whole island was under British rule until 1922, when it was divided into two sections. Belfast is the capital city of Northern Ireland, and Dublin is the capital of the Republic. Of the five million people living on the island of Ireland, one and a half million live in Northern Ireland.

Dublin is Ireland's largest city, with one-third of the population living there. It is an old city dating back to the Viking period and was built on the River Liffey.

Above, the Irish flag
Right, market day in Macroom, county Cork
Opposite, Macroom is a colorful Irish town

The most important commercial and industrial city in the country, its seaport handles half of the foreign trade of the Republic. Despite its industrial background, Dublin is an attractive city with many historic buildings. Christ Church and St. Patrick's Cathedral were both built in the 12th century, and the city's oldest college, Trinity, was founded in 1591. The Custom House and Four Courts buildings are wonderful examples of 18th century **architecture**.

IRISH

Ireland is the only nation to have a musical instrument, the harp, as its national emblem.

Above, stone carving on the Chapel Royal of Dublin Castle
Right, close view of a Celtic stone carving

Dublin has become famous for the architecture that was designed during the reign of King George V. **Georgian** doors and door knobs can still be found on houses sur-rounding many public parks in Dublin.

Ireland's larger towns often have a main square where a weekly market is held. Narrow streets are typical since most towns developed in a time when donkeys and carts were the main form of transportation.

Brightly painted buildings and preserved ancient architecture are common in Ireland. Many villages are famous for their stunning buildings.

Pubs are the center of city and village life, and most people visit them at least several times a week to meet friends and discuss their daily lives.

IRISH CLIFFS

The Cliffs of Moher on the west coast of Ireland are over five miles (8 km) long and 650 feet (200 m) high, making them the longest cliffs in all of Europe.

IRISH SPORTS

Gaelic football and hurling are two traditional Irish sports. Hurling is played with a small ball and wooden stick. Gaelic football is similar to soccer, except the ball can be held.

An example of the detailed stone carving found on Adare Manor

IRISH

Several old abbeys, or church buildings, are used as schools in Ireland today. Kylemore Abbey in Connemara National Park is one of the most well-known.

IRISH
FUEL

Peat land, or bogs, which cover 15 per-cent of the Irish landscape, has been the main source of fuel in this nation for hundreds of years.

Ruins of Kilcrea Friary, a place where Irish monks once lived

Ireland is a **democracy**. The government provides medical care and education to all citizens. In 1990, the first female president was elected. Northern Ireland is still governed by England.

Citizens have the freedom to practice any religion they choose. Ninety-four percent of the people in the Republic are Catholic, while the remainder are mostly Protestant. In Northern Ireland 70 percent are Protestant and 30 percent are Catholic. Churches play a major role in the lives of most Irish people.

IRISH
RIVER

The River Shannon, the longest river in Ireland, flows 240 miles (386 km) before emptying into the Atlantic Ocean.

Above, stone crucifix sculpture at Mount Mellerayin in county Waterford, Ireland Left, Belfast City Cathedral in Belfast, Northern Ireland

IRISH
GLASS

Waterford crystal is one of Ireland's most famous exports. The skill of the glassmakers is recognized all over the world.

A rooster (below) can be found on virtually every Irish farmstead (right) Opposite, thatched cottage in county Limerick

Ireland was an Irish-speaking nation until the 16th century. Since then the language declined, and now the vast majority of people speak English. The country is officially **bilingual**, so all school children are required to learn Irish. Only three percent of the people speak it on a daily basis, living in Irish areas called **Gaeltachs** (Irish speaking).

The Aran Islands, three small islands located off the west coast, attract large numbers of visitors. There people speak traditional Irish.

IRISH
TOLLS

Above, Giant's Causeway in county Antrim
Right, Cliffs of Moher in county Clare

The biggest island, Inishmore, is only eight miles (13 km) long and two miles (3 km) wide. Although small, these islands contain several prehistoric stone forts and old churches dating back to the fifth century. The landscape is mostly exposed limestone, with little soil for growing crops. Islanders gather sea-weed and mix it with sand to create soil. The eastern side of the islands is low-lying, rising towards the west where tall, sheer cliffs are found.

THE ECONOMY

The population of Ireland in the 19th century was eight million, and the potato was the main food source. Between 1845 and 1848, a **blight** destroyed the potato crop, causing more than one million people to die from starvation and disease. During this period and the following years, thousands of people decided to emigrate to countries such as America, England, and Australia.

Leprechaun crossing

The Great Potato **Famine**, as it was called, was the worst natural disaster to occur in all of Ireland's long history. Today, Ireland still relies mainly on agriculture, but only a small percentage of the work force is involved in agriculture. The typical farm is family-owned and covers less than 100 acres (250 ha). Cattle and crops are raised on the lowlands; sheep often graze on the mountainsides and along the rocky coasts.

Above, signs such as this one delight tourists Center, "Festival of the Boats" in county Galway

As an island, Ireland has long depended on the sea for food and for transporting goods. Ireland has a large fishing fleet, but overfishing has led to a decline of this industry. The electronics and chemical industries are now the biggest employers, and many foreign companies are now moving to Ireland to take advantage of the nation's young and highly educated workers.

IRISH POWER

Major industries in Ireland are run by the government. They include steel, chemicals, sugar, and electrical power industries, as well as public transportation.

IRISH SWANS

An Irish legend tells that King Lir's children were turned into swans. To this day, it is illegal to kill swans in Ireland.

IRISH
FIND

Discoveries of natural gas deposits in county Cork have lessened the nation's dependence on oil from other countries.

IRISH
MUSIC

Ireland is a nation that loves traditional music and instruments. The violin was named "fiddle" by Irish musicians.

Right, decorated shop front in Cork city Opposite, heather and gorse, two kinds of Irish wildflowers, growing by an ancient stone wall

THE PAST AND THE FUTURE

The **folklore** of Ireland is full of stories about fairies and leprechauns. Centuries ago, it was believed that fairies lived under mounds of earth and that touching one brought bad luck. The most famous folklore is that of leprechauns. Legend tells that if a person catches a leprechaun, he must lead his captor to a pot of gold. But one glance away from him, and the leprechaun would vanish. Today many people still tell these ancient legends to their children.

I reland holds a special place in the hearts of people all over the world because so many have **ancestors** who came from this small island. Whether visitors are retracing their roots or visiting on a vacation, they will remember Ireland for its friendly people, unique villages, and a landscape painted with ancient mystery and wonder.

Glossary

Ancestors are relatives from whom a person is descended: grandparents, great-grandparents, and so on.

Architecture is the design and construction of buildings.

Astronomical calendars mark the position of the moon and stars in the sky at various times of the year.

A person is **bilingual** if he or she can speak two languages.

The potato **blight** was a disease that caused potatoes to spoil in the ground, causing a food shortage.

Bogs are areas of soft, naturally waterlogged ground where peat is formed.

A country's **climate** is the average weather determined over a number of years.

A **democracy** is a form of government in which a nation's leaders are elected by the people of that nation.

The **European Community** is a group of countries in western Europe who joined together to improve trade and commerce.

A **famine** is a food shortage that causes people to suffer from starvation and sometimes die from lack of food.

The traditional beliefs of a group of people which are passed on to new generations by storytelling are called **folklore**.

Gaeltachs are areas where the traditional Irish language is still spoken as the main language of the people.

When something is referred to as **Georgian**, it means it was built during the time King George V ruled England.

Megaliths are Stone Age structures made of large stones; they are found mainly in western Europe.

The **United Kingdom**, or UK for short, consists of England, Scotland, Wales, and Northern Ireland; the ruler, or Head of State, is the King or Queen of England.

Vikings were raiders from Scandinavia who attacked western Europe in the years between the 8th and the 10th centuries.

Index